YES I HAVE ADHD. DEAL. \

Copyright © 2022 by Yes I Have Anxiety, Inc.

All rights reserved.

Thank you for purchasing an authorized edition of this book and for complying with copyright laws by not reproducing, scanning, or distributing any part of it in any form without permission.

Consumer Use Disclaimer: The "Yes I Have" book series was created in light-hearted, relatable fun to create distractions from things individuals may be dealing with. All "Yes I Have" books are not intended to diagnose medical conditions nor provide a cure for any medical conditions. This book is not meant to be a replacement for real medical intervention if needed.

ISBN: 979-8-9854677-9-6
First Edition: March 2022
Yes I Have Anxiety, Inc.
Grove, Ok 74345

WHAT ARE YOU DEALING WITH?
WE GOT YOU!

Visit www.YesIHave.com for more books!

Do you have an idea for the next "Yes I Have®" book? Reach out to us through our website!

You might just see your idea in a future book!

What are you dealing with?

Color This Square Blue	Draw a Smiley Face
Draw a Star	Color the Beach Ball
Color the Flower	Draw a Sun

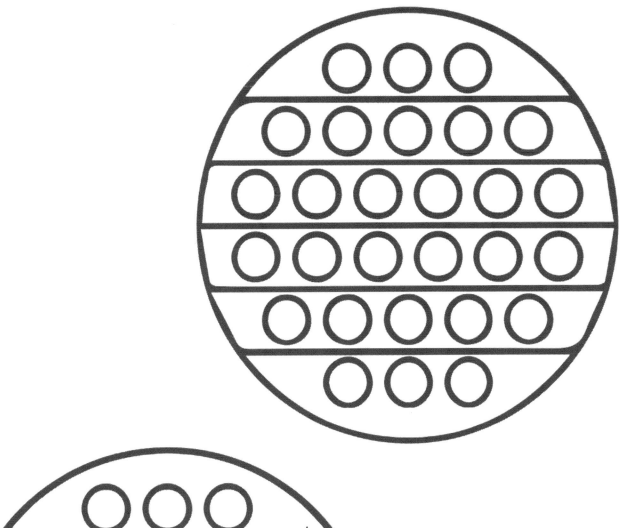
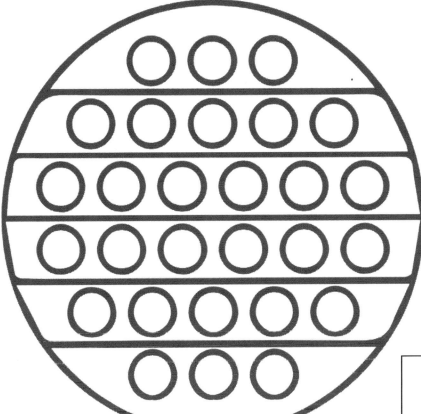

Design Cool Bubble Poppers!

Put Braces on the Teeth!

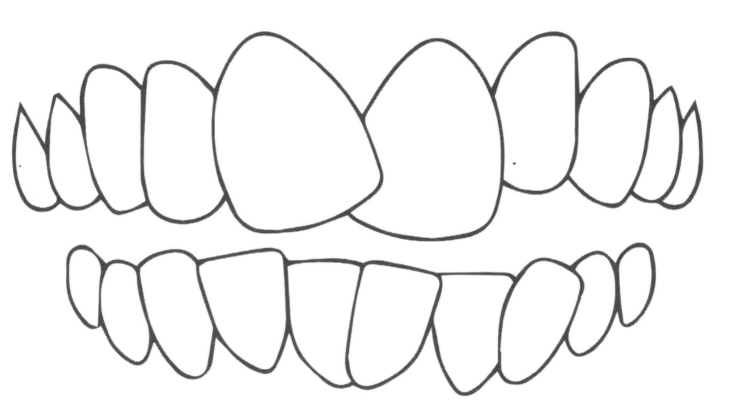

1. Connect the Dots!

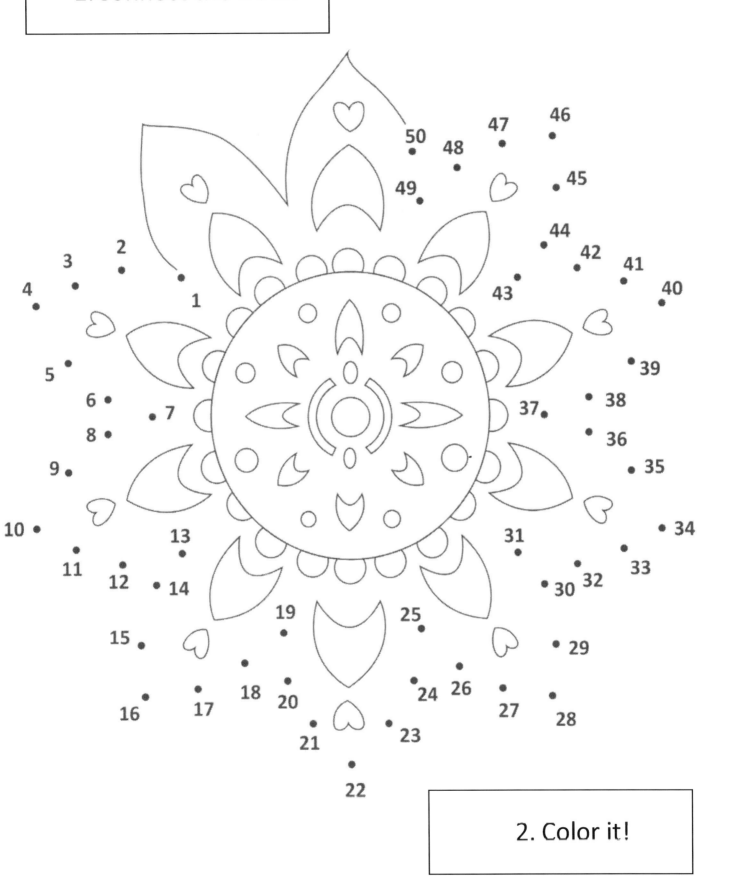

2. Color it!

Mix up the Cube!

Now Solve it!

Write the First Thing That Comes to Your Mind When You Read These Colors!

Orange

_____

Blue

_____

Pink

_____

White

_____

Yellow

_____

Purple

_____

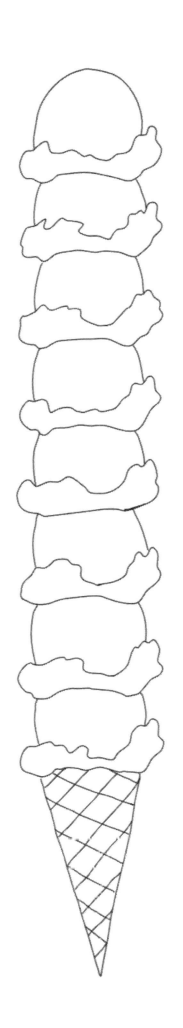

We All Scream for Ice-cream!

P.S. Highlight These X's!

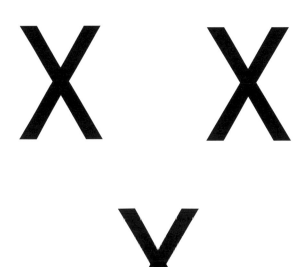

Picture Find!

What Color are Your Eyes?

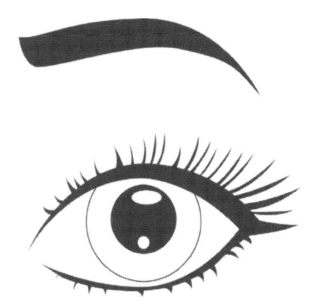

What Color do You Wish they Were?

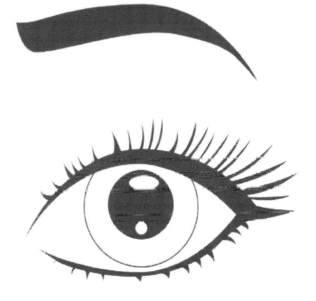

This Page Needs Glitter.
Enough Said.

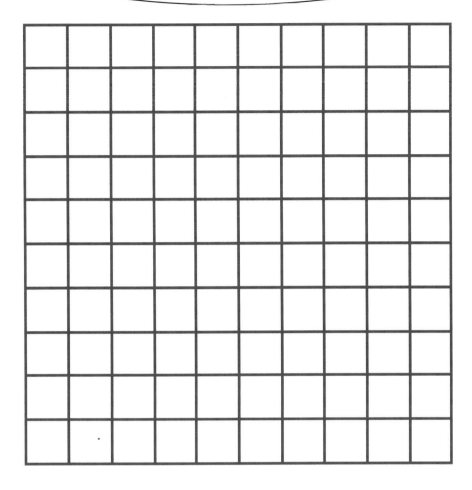

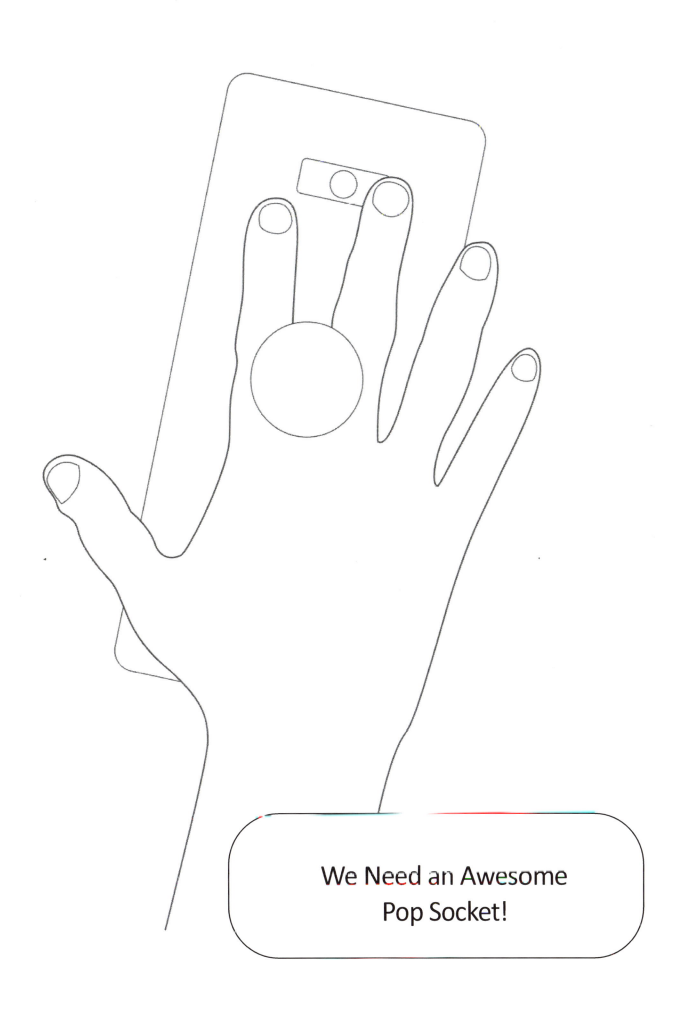

Make this Square EXTRA	Make a Checkered Flag 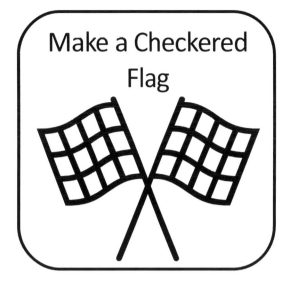
Color the Grapes 	Black out This Square
Fill with Circles	Change to an Up Arrow 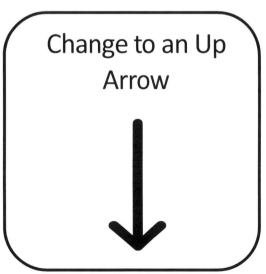

Fix the Unibrows!

Solve it!

5	3			7				
6			1	9	5			
	9	8					6	
8				6				3
4			8		3			1
7				2				6
	6					2	8	
			4	1	9			5
				8			7	9

Look, It's a Butterfly!

Fill Up the Brain With all Your Thoughts!

Color By Number!

1 = Blue   2 = Yellow   3 = Red

Doodle all Over This Page!

Create Unique Fingerprints!

Example

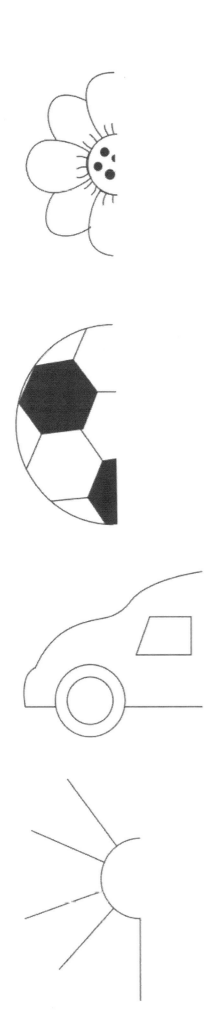

Complete the Other Half!

Trace Your Hands on This Page!

Color the Caterpillar 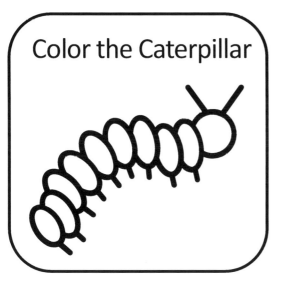	**This Square Needs Glitter**
Draw a Moon	**Color This Square Orange**
Draw a Heart	**Color the Stars** 

#SQUIRREL
#SQUIRREL

#JustColorIt

Copy & Paste!

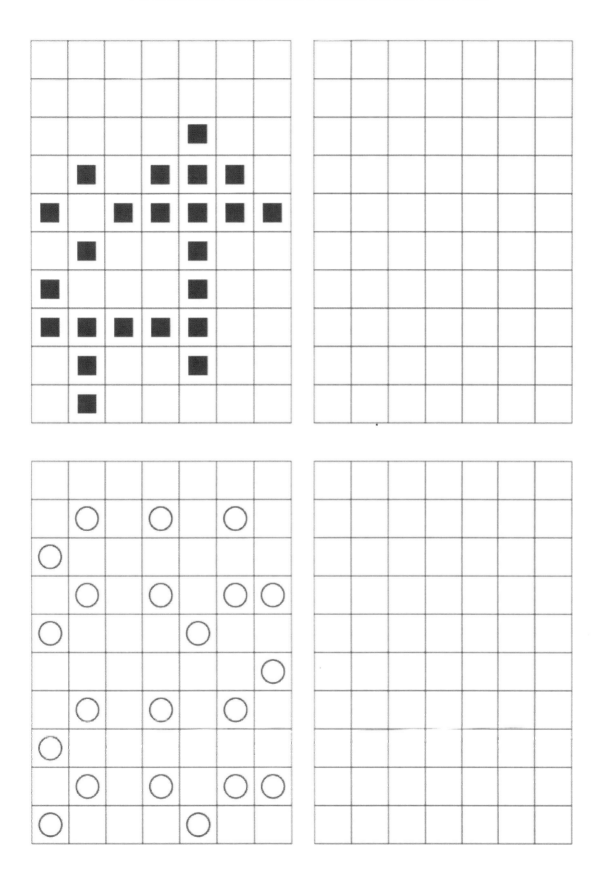

Go NUTS Making These Donuts Pretty!

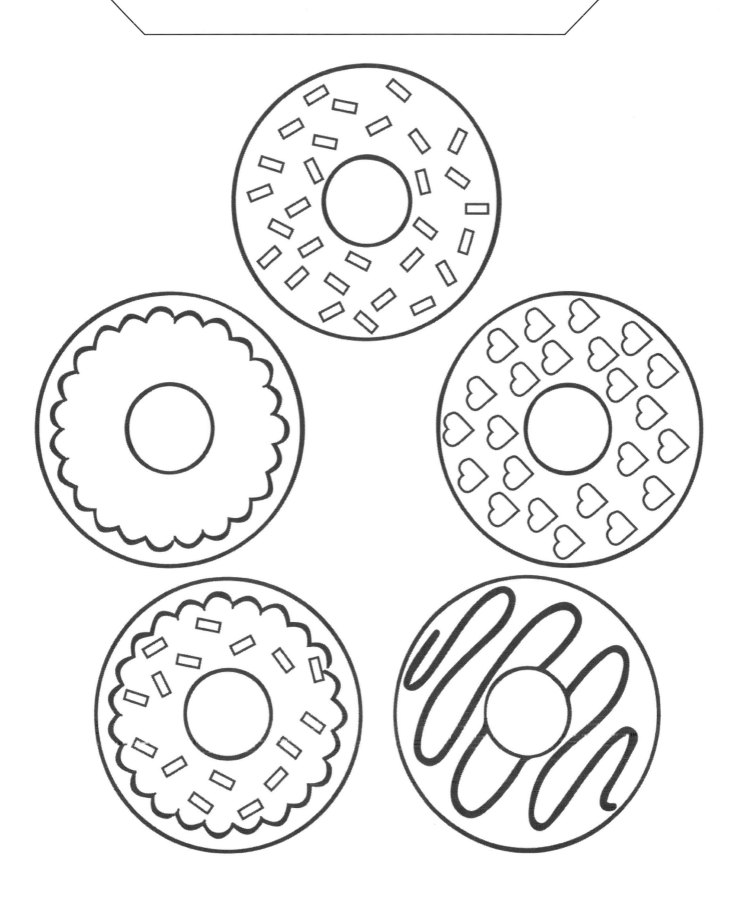

Continue the Lines!

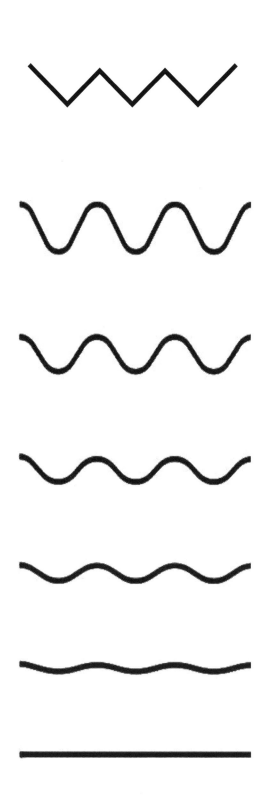

Make the Rocket Blast Off!

```
R O C K E T S H I P
A H B O Q Z H S U H
S C L R O K G P Q D
T V A B R B Z A C V
R L S I B C B C C V
O Q T T E W Z E R S
N M O S T A R S W H
A O F R G M L S X P
U O F E F S T J I S
T N G L A U N C H Y
```

Rocketship   Blast Off   Launch   Space
Stars   Orbit   Astronaut   Moon

Add What is Missing to Each Frame to Make them all Complete!

Color the Black Keys 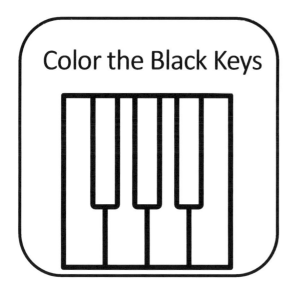	**Write Your Name**
Make This Square Red	**This Square is a Minimalist**
Give this Shirt Stripes 	**The Spider Needs a Web** 

We Challenge You to Make This Page as MESSY as Possible!

Give the Lady Bugs Their Spots!

No Rules on This Page!

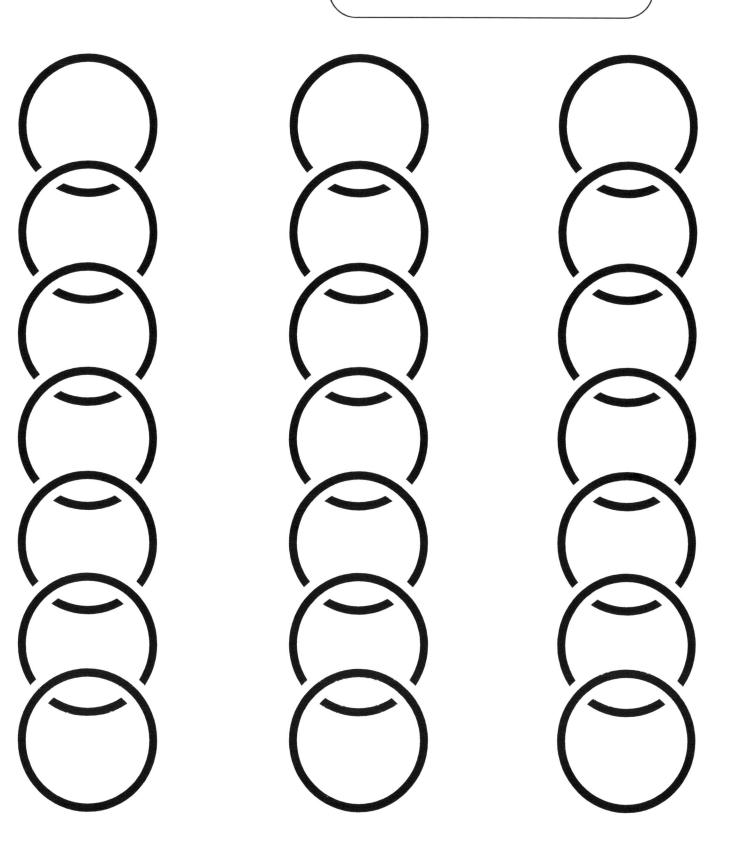

Put Mud Stains All Over the Shirt!

Draw a Lightning Bolt	Scribble in This Square
Color the Cupcake 	Color This Square Red
Draw a Cloud	Color the Ball Black 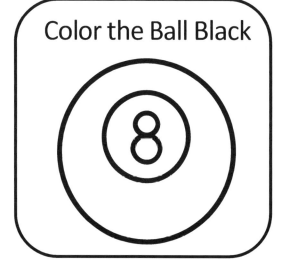

Make Him Cool!

Oh, Look a Maze!

Make the Squares Different Shades of Grey!

1   3   6
Light   Medium   Dark

1	2	3
4	5	6

Sign This Page Over and Over. Use a Different Style Each Time!

Finish Each Leaf!

Flower Cookies Make by a Professional:

VS.

Flower Cookies Make by YOU:

Make a Design out of Q-Tips on This Page!

Set a Timer! How Fast Can You Finish This Page?

7 + 0 = ☐	9 + 7 = ☐
7 + 1 = ☐	8 + 7 = ☐
7 + 2 = ☐	7 + 7 = ☐
7 + 3 = ☐	6 + 7 = ☐
7 + 4 = ☐	5 + 7 = ☐
7 + 5 = ☐	4 + 7 = ☐
7 + 6 = ☐	3 + 7 = ☐
7 + 7 = ☐	2 + 7 = ☐
7 + 8 = ☐	1 + 7 = ☐
7 + 9 = ☐	0 + 7 = ☐

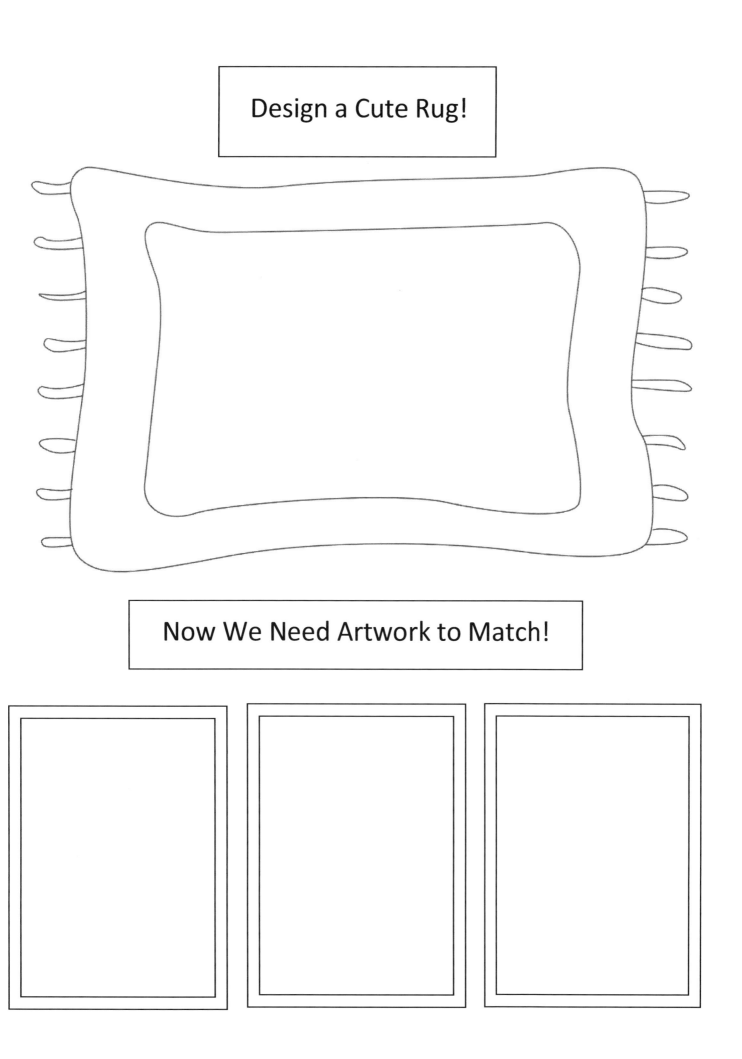

Build a House Out of Spaghetti Noodles on This Page!

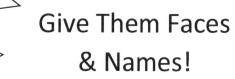

Give Them Faces & Names!

Draw a Spiral	Color the Bubbles 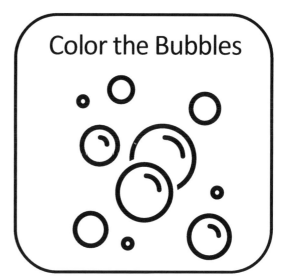
Make it Rain 	Highlight the X 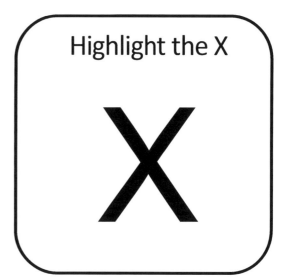
What is Your Lucky Number?	Just Color it 

Start in the Top Corner of the Page. Put Your Pen Down and Let it Take You Where It Wants to Go.

DON'T LIFT THE PEN UNTIL YOU'RE DONE.

Don't miss out on FREE books and New Book Announcements!!!

Follow us on our social media platforms to be included in weekly giveaways, book tour location announcements, new book releases, and videos for page idea inspiration!!!

officialyesihave

yesihaveofficial

Yes I Have Books

Yes I Have Official

JOIN OUR NEWSLETTER!:
Text
YESIHAVE
To 22828 to get started!

Hey Fans!! If you post your page videos on social media and one goes viral, we want to know! Send your video to us at yesihavebooks@gmail.com

We showcase our viral fan videos on our website and social media outlets! We have 100+ viral videos and counting!

Want to Find More Books?

Scan the QR Code, Then Decorate it!

Mood Swings Perfectionism
Kids Anxiety Stress Ideas
Hard Times Pets Boredom
Baby Fever Christmas Fever

Made in the USA
Las Vegas, NV
30 October 2022